Introduction

To our friends the Ball family; Liz, Tony Alex and Jessica

Magic Sparkles have been used on the cakes in this book. They are edible and safe to use on any cake decorating
They can be used on cakes, sweets, chocolates or desserts for a special touch.
Use straight from the pot or grind down to a finer glitter. To do this, either leave in the pot and stir with a teaspoon handle or use a pestle and mortar. To attach to cakes the surface should be tacky not wet - if too wet they will dissolve. Edible glue - see recipe below, is ideal although you can use water or alcohol. Their appearance is enhanced by good lighting - halogen or spotlights work well.

How To Use The Size Guide (CC)

On any instructions for modelling in this book I have used the Cel Cakes Size Guide. This should make it easier to produce proportioned figures. To achieve the correct size, the ball of paste should sit in the correct hole (size below it) with 1/3 of the paste showing out of the bottom and 2/3 out of the top (this does not apply to the smallest sizes). You will then have approximately the correct size ball of paste to shape.

Recipes

Modelling Paste

Either:- $1/2$ sugarpaste, $1/2$ flower paste kneaded together, or knead 5ml (1tsp) of gum tragacanth into 225g (8ozs) sugarpaste and leave for 8 hours, or knead 5ml (1tsp) Tylo (CMC) powder into 225g (8ozs) sugarpaste.

Mexican Paste

Mix together 225g (8ozs) of icing sugar and 3 level teaspoons of gum tragacanth. Add 25ml (5tsp) of cold water (taken from tap). Mix together, turnout and knead well. Store in a plastic bag and a sealed container for 6-8 hours to mature. The paste will feel very hard but will soften up easily. Break off small pieces and soften in your fingers. Matured paste will freeze.

Royal Icing

Place 30ml (6 level tsp) of merriwhite in a mixing bowl and gradually add 5tbs cold water mixing with a wooden spoon until free from lumps. Add 225g (8ozs) of icing sugar and mix until smooth. Add 110g (4ozs) of icing sugar and then add the rest gradually until the correct consistency is reached. Beat well for approximately 5 minutes. Store in the fridge, in an airtight container. It should keep for 4 weeks.

Softened Sugarpaste

Place the amount of sugarpaste you want to soften in a bowl. Chop up roughly and then gradually add drops of cold water. Break down with a fork or a spoon and mix until smooth and lump free. Continue until required consistency is reached. The first time you do this, be careful not to add too much water too soon. It softens quickly.

Edible Glue

This is easily made with 1 part Tylo (CMC) powder to 25-30 parts water. Place the powder in a bottle or jar that has a lid. Add the water, replace the lid and shake. There will be thick creamy white pieces in the water. They will dissolve and the liquid will become clear by the following day.

Edible Supports

(for modelled figures). These are easily made from any left over Mexican paste. Roll out long thin sausage pieces and cut different lengths. Leave to dry for at least six hours. When used in modelled figures they are a safe alternative to cocktail sticks etc.

NOTE: **ANY SPECIAL EQUIPMENT USED HAS A SUPPLIER CODE. FOR EXAMPLE – SIZE GUIDE (CC) – SUPPLIER CEL CAKES.
SEE ACKNOWLEDGMENTS PAGE 37 .**

Shoes and Bags

18cm (7in), 12.5cm (5in) & 7.5cm (3in) cakes marzipanned and iced in Icecraft sugarpaste, 4 madeira cakes 11cm x 5cm, 16in cake board, 12.5cm (5in) & 7.5cm (3in) cake cards, 3k (6lb 10z) sugarpaste, 450g (1lb) mexican paste, royal icing, 2 pots of white magic sparkles ground finer (p1) (BK), apricot jam or buttercream, Trex, edible glue (p1), isopropyl alcohol.

Paste Colours: Pink, Ice blue, Grape Violet (SF).

Dust Colours: Carnation, Mauve, Speedwell (SC).

Spray Colour: Pearl (PME).

Handbag cutter (SB), shoe cutter (CC), heel mould (CC), styrofoam hen egg (CC), car body repair mesh (Halfords) (used as a former to dry shoes over), quilting embosser (PC), butterfly set (PC), shoes, bags & confetti set (PC), ladies accessory set (FMM), medium heart cutter from set of 3 (FMM), calyx cutters (FMM), large blossom (FMM), posy pick, diamantes and crystals on wires (CP), double heart cutter (Jem), bow cutters size 1 & 2 (Jem), silver wires size 24, no.42 nozzle, 6 lengths of dowelling, non stick rolling pin and board, pastry brush, no.2 paintbrush, greaseproof paper.

1 Keep a ¼ of mexican paste white and colour each other ¼ pink, lilac and blue. Follow instructions with the shoe and bag cutters to make 1 shoe and one bag in each colour. Choose a theme for each colour i.e. Pink bag and shoe – hearts, lilac – bows, blue – blossoms and butterflies, white – quilting and calyx flowers with diamante centres. Leave to dry.

2 Cover cake board with sugarpaste. Place cakes on cards and board. Push 3 pieces of dowelling into 18cm & 12.5cm cakes down to the boards. Mark level with top of cake, remove dowelling and trim. Push dowelling back into cakes so they are level with icing. Stack the cakes.

3 Place no.42 nozzle in a piping bag with royal icing and pipe scrolls around base of each cake.

4 Grease a non stick rolling board with trex. Grease the small heart, bow, blossom and butterfly with trex. Roll out coloured mexican paste thinly – do not lift and turn. Cut out shapes and attach to each tier with a little glue.

5 Spray the three tiers with pearl lustre. Using a pastry brush, apply glue thinly to the iced board. Cover with magic sparkles.

6 Roll out mexican paste and cut out 2 each of butterflies, shoes, bags, hearts and flowers. Brush one of each shape thinly with glue then place a wire up the centre to half way. Cover the wire with the matching shape and leave to dry.

7 Spread jam over each of the small madeira cakes and cover with sugarpaste. Emboss the sides with small cutters and one with the quilting embosser. Roll out sugarpaste large enough to fit over the top of the cakes plus 2cm extra on each side. Trim straight and cut a square out of each corner measuring 1.5cm. Place icing over cake, join corners together and smooth. Leave to dry.

8 Mix isopropyl alcohol with powder colours to a very thin consistency. Paint embossing on each shoe box. Position, shoe boxes, shoes, bags and shapes on wires close together on greaseproof paper. Spray liberally with pearl lustre spray. Leave to dry. Turn over or around where needed and spray again.

9 Position shoe boxes evenly around cake and secure with a little royal icing towards the back bottom corners. Attach the shoes and bags with royal icing. Push posy pick into top tier. Fill with mexican paste and push shapes on wires, diamantes and crystals into the pick. Trim wires to correct length were necessary.

Wedding Car

25.5cm (10in) and 15cm (6in) marzipanned round rich fruit cakes, 33cm (13in) cake board, 15cm (6in) cake card, 1.8kg (4lb) Icecraft sugarpaste, flower paste, royal icing, magic sparkles hint colours: pink, blue and lilac all ground finer (p1), isopropyl alcohol, edible glue (p1), trex. Food Colouring Pen Black (SF).

Paste Colours: Pink, Black, Ice Blue, Grape violet (SF)

Powder Colours: Silver, Snowflake (SK), Kingfisher, Black, Mauve, Carnation, Caramel, Peach (SC).

Spray Colour: Pearl (PME).

Wedding car mould (Karen Davies), small heart cutters (FMM), confetti cutters from shoe & handbag set (PC), no.1 piping nozzle, paintbrushes, silver wires, 3 pieces of dowelling.

1   Place cakes on cake boards. Cover cakes with sugarpaste. Emboss immediately around cake sides. Push the 3 pieces of dowelling into the centre of the large cake approximately 7cm apart. Use a food colouring pen to mark the height of the cake top on the dowelling. Remove dowelling and cut with a serrated knife. Push the trimmed dowelling back into the cake.

2   Place small cake on top of large cake. Use royal icing and a no.1 piping nozzle to pipe a small plain shell around base of both cakes. Mix isopropyl alcohol with powder colours and paint embossed shapes. Spray pearl lustre all over both cakes.

3   Colour 3 small pieces of flower paste pink, lilac and blue. Cut out small hearts in each colour and sandwich together over half lengths of silver wire with glue. Leave to dry. You will need approximately 5 lenghts of wire with 2 pairs of hearts on each. Leave to dry.

4   Dust the car mould with a little icing sugar or cornflour. Spread around the mould then turn over and tap out the excess. Knead a piece of flower paste then roll into a thick flat shape to fit into the mould easier. Press into the mould trimming any excess paste away. Turn mould over and bend slightly to release the car. Twist a cocktail stick into the bottom centre of each tyre – or leave to dry then place a cocktail stick half way up each tyre, spread glue over stick and surrounding paste, then cover with flower paste and leave to dry.

5   Attach a small piece of flower paste to the back of the car with edible glue (to insert wires later). Turn car over. Dust faces with peach powder, cheeks with pink, brides veil with snowflake and headdress pink. Mix isopropyl alcohol with brown powder and

paint hair. Dust brides headdress and veil with snowflake. Dip a cocktail stick into black paste colour and mark eyes. Paint grooms suit grey or black and dickie bow blue.

6   Brush hearts on wires with glue then cover with magic sparkles. Trim to length required. Push cocktail sticks from car wheels into top of cake. Push hearts on wires into flower paste at back of the car. Shape 5 tin cans from flower paste and attach to top of cake. Strings from the bumper to the cans can be piped and painted but they can break when the cake is moved. Instead attach pieces of grey cotton with royal icing from the bumper to the cans keeping it loose between the two. Paint bumper and horseshoe silver. Add a little black powder to the silver powder to paint the back of the car seat. Use the food colouring pen to write 'Mr & Mrs' on the number plate.

Gerberas

20cm (8in) marzipanned cake placed on a 30.5cm (12in) cake board, 1kg (2¼lb) Icecraft sugarpaste, Mexican paste, royal icing, 2 pots of hint of lemon magic sparkles ground finer (BK), Trex, isopropyl alcohol, edible glue (p1).

Paste Colour: **Primrose, Ruby, Grape Violet, Peach, Black (SF)**

Powder Colour: **Silver, Moonbeams in Sapphire, Topaz and Ruby (SK)**

Daisy / gerbera cutter 70mm (PME), daisy marguerite plunger cutter – small (PME), daisy chain cutter (PC), size guide (CC), no.2 piping nozzle, pastry brush, soft sponge, fine paintbrush, tin foil.

1 Place cake on board. Colour 950g of sugarpaste lemon. Cover cake then board. Use a pastry brush to cover board thinly and evenly with glue. Cover with magic sparkles.

2 Colour some Mexican paste lilac, peach and pink. Cut 6 pieces of tin foil to 8cm square. Place 2 pieces together and make 3 shallow cups to dry flowers in. They will look good if left slightly uneven. Roll out Mexican paste and cut 2 sets of petals for each flower. Dust ruby powder over the pink flower, topaz over the peach and sapphire over the lilac. Attach one set of petals over another using glue to secure. Lay each flower in a foil cup to dry.

3 Roll out coloured Mexican paste thinly and cut out approximately 24 small daisies in each colour. Press out onto sponge to cup the flower. Leave to dry. Attach around base of cake with a little royal icing. Mix isopropyl alcohol with silver powder and paint centre of small daisies.

4 Make a centre for the large daisies by rolling a size 10 ball of lemon sugarpaste, flattening slightly and attaching. Brush centres thinly with glue and cover with magic sparkles. Lay on top of cake to check position then mark top and bottom of flower stem (approximately 6cm) with a cocktail stick. Remove flowers and scratch 3 straight lines as a guide for piping the stems.

5 Colour a little Mexican paste grey. Grease a non stick rolling board and the daisy cutter with trex. Roll out the grey Mexican paste and cut out 6 leaves. Colour a little royal icing grey and place in a piping bag with a no.2 nozzle. Pipe stems then attach flowers and leaves. Colour 50g of sugarpaste grey. For each pot, use a size 13 ball of sugarpaste. Shape and attach to cake. Add a strip of paste around the top edge of pot.

6 Mix silver powder colour with isopropyl alcohol and paint stem, leaves and pots.

25.5cm x 12.5cm (10in x 5in) Rich fruit or sponge cake, 900g (2lb) marzipan, 900g (2lb) Regalice, 35cm x 25.5cm (14in x 10in) oblong cake board, mexican paste (p1), a little royal icing, isopropyl alcohol, Trex, edible glue (p1).

Paste Colours: Girl, Rose, Violet, Daffodil, Vine. Boy, Vine, Gentian, Violet, Chestnut (light for soles, darker for beer, then darkest for shoes) (SK). Flesh colour for both cakes is a little rose and chestnut mixed together.

Powder Colours: Girl & Boy, Flesh and Silver.

White Hologram glitter (EA), large and small number cutters (PC), non stick rolling pin and board, sharp scalpel, no.2 piping nozzle, fine paintbrush.

1   Ice cake in chosen colour, ice the board in white.

2   Use pattern from p35. Cut pattern into individual pieces.

3   Grease a non-stick rolling board with Trex and roll out flesh coloured mexican paste. Do not lift the paste as you roll out. Lightly grease the rolled out paste with Trex before laying on the pattern. Use a fine sharp scalpel to cut around shape. Lift and stick on to the cake with edible glue. Repeat with all other colours and patterns. Do not worry at this stage if your adjoining pieces do not meet exactly - the silver line will hide this, so remember any gaps should be no bigger than a piped line.

4   Mix the royal icing with a little silver powder. Pipe the outline. Pipe the name. Leave to dry then mix silver powder with alcohol and paint outlines and name. Any gaps between pieces should now be unnoticeable.

5   Grease board with Trex and roll out white Mexican paste. Do not lift. Grease the number cutters and cut out one large 18 and four small 18's. Lift on to a sponge pad and leave to dry.

6   Using sugarpaste roll one sausage in cake colour and two in white, they should be the same length as the cake and 1cm or under in diameter. Only roll out enough to fit one side at a time. When it is almost the width you

require roll with a smoother to give an even finish. Twist the three together into a rope and attach to the cake base with edible glue. Repeat for other three sides. Leave to dry and then paint one of the white strands silver.

7   Paint the numbers with glue and then dip them into White Hologram. Leave them to dry and then attach them to cake, large 18 on cake top, small 18's on each corner of rope trim.

Butterfly

20cm (8in) marzipanned and iced (in Icecraft sugarpaste) cake on a 30cm (12in) board, modelling paste (p1), 225g (8oz) sugarpaste, mexican paste, white magic sparkles (BK), edible glue (p1), royal icing, isopropyl alcohol, Trex.

Paste Colours: Black, Mint Green, Ice Blue, Pink, Egg Yellow, Grape Violet, Peach (SF). Dust Colours: Silver, Snowflake (SK)

Spray Colour: Blue, Pearl (PME)

Butterfly cutter (PC), mouth / veining tool (Jem), straight frill cutter from set 5-8 (FMM), blossom set and large blossom set (FMM), no.2 piping nozzle.

1 To spray the blue sky on the cake, make sure that the can is moving side to side and up and down as you begin to spray. This will prevent an intense blast of colour in one place and will give a softer, cloudier appearance. Spray all over with the pearl. Clean the board

2 Colour sugarpaste green and ice the board.

3 Trace and cut out the butterfly pattern on p32. Lay on top of the cake and mark with a cocktail stick or knife.

4 Colour 5 pieces of mexican paste pink, lilac, blue, yellow and peach. Cut out approximately 36 small blossoms in each colour. Cut out 2 large blossoms in pink and emboss each petal with a small blossom, and cut out 2 medium in each of the other colours.

5 Colour some mexican paste grey. Grease a non stick board and the butterfly cutter with trex. Roll out the paste and cut out 12 butterflies. Lay 7 over a piece of folded card and attach 5 flat around the cake.

6 Soften some green sugarpaste with water (p1) and place in a piping bag. Pipe grass around bottom edge of cake and attach groups of blossoms.

7 Roll out lilac mexican paste and use the butterfly pattern to cut out top half of wings. Attach to cake with edible glue. Roll out pieces of coloured mexican paste and use the frill cutter to cut strips of paste approximately 1.4cm wide. Attach to lower half of wings matching up edges and trimming at sides to fit. Attach different coloured blossoms into blossom holes. Spray lower wings with pearl.

8 Grind the pot of magic sparkles finer (p1). Brush edible glue thinly over top half of wings and cover with magic sparkles. Attach large blossoms in the middle of wings and medium blossoms to top half. Attach small blossoms around edges of wings.

9 Colour a little royal icing grey and using a no.2 nozzle pipe antennae. Using the size guide (p1), colour a size 14 ball of sugarpaste grey. Divide in half. Shape one half into a long thin pointed body and attach. Shape the other half into a ball and flatten slightly for the head.

10 Attach folded butterflies to the cake using a little royal icing. Paint all small butterflies and large butterflies head, body and antennae silver by mixing the powder colour with isopropyl alcohol. Mark mouth with the mouth embosser and eyes with a cocktail stick dipped into black paste colour.

11 Brush all blossoms with a little snowflake lustre and then paint a small silver centre.

25cm x 20cm (10 x 8in) Marzipanned oval rich fruit cake, 36cm x 30cm (14in x 12in) cake board, 1.8kg (4lb) Icecraft sugarpaste, 175g (6oz) mexican paste, royal icing, 450g (1lb) modelling paste, 1 pot hint of pink Magic Sparkles (BK), edible glue (p1), Trex.

Paste Colours: **Ruby (pink)**, grape violet, egg yellow, black (SF).

Dust Colours: Carnation, Mauve, Buttercup, Marigold, Black, white (SC) Snowflake Lustre (SK)
Spray Colour: **Pearl (PME)**

Basketweave embosser, quilting embosser, teddies from make a cradle set, lace from patchwork squares, duck & bricks from nursery set, gift tag (PC), life size baby bootie cutter (Jem), bow cutters size 1 & 3 (Jem), mouth / veining tool (Jem), stitch wheel / dresden tool (PME), 2cm double closed curve serrated crimper (PME), black food colouring pen, smoother, paintbrushes, ball or bone tool.

1. Place cake on board and cover with sugarpaste. Emboss immediately with the basketweave embosser.

2. Colour 225g sugarpaste pink and ice board. Emboss with small teddy.

3. With a little trex on the work surface and your hands, roll 2 sausages of modelling paste with a diameter of approximately 7.5mm. Lay the two pieces side by side and use a smoother to roll and make even. Twist together and trim to a length of approximately 12cm. Fold into ½ a circle and leave to dry. Make two.

4. Roll 3 longer sausages of modelling paste for the top rope edge. You can make this rope in 2 halves and place the joins were the handles will be. Make a longer rope and attach around the base of the cake. Attach handles with royal icing covering rope joins.

Spray cake sides, handles and board with pearl lustre.

5. Grease the palm of your hand lightly with trex and roll thin whiskers from tiny balls of mexican paste. Leave to dry.

6. Colour 140g of sugarpaste violet. Using the size guide (p1) shape half an oval for the rabbits's body from a size 16 ball of sugarpaste. Attach to cake with glue. Run the stitch wheel over centre of body from front to back. Shape arms each from size 12, attach and mark down sides with the stitch wheel. Shape head from a size 16, pointing slightly towards nose area. Mark centre of face with stitch wheel, mark mouth with the mouth tool and add a small pink nose. Indent holes for eyes with the paintbrush handle. Shape ears each from a size 13 and attach.

7. Colour a small piece of modelling paste black with the paste colour and roll 2 small balls for eyes. Push into holes and smooth with a ball tool. Mix snowflake powder with isopropyl alcohol and paint a small highlight into each eye. Soften a size 14 ball of sugarpaste with water (p1) and place in a piping bag. Pipe over rabbits body and arms, then spread out with a damp paintbrush. When covered 'dab' at icing with the paintbrush to give fur effect. Repeat over head and ears. Make a small hole with a cocktail stick and insert whiskers.

8. Colour some mexican paste pink and cut out booties as per instructions with cutter. When you cut out the top front section, do

CONTINUED...

not roll the paste too thin because when you attach to the sole it could loose its shape. Emboss the front section with the small teddy. Stick booties together and leave to dry. Spray front of shoe with pearl lustre.

9   Brush edible glue around back of booties and cover with sparkles.

10   Grease a non stick rolling board and the lace cutter with trex. Roll out mexican paste thinly – do not lift and turn. Cut out strips of lace. Remove small pieces with a cocktail stick. Dust with snowflake lustre and attach around back sections of booties.

11   Roll out mexican paste and cut out the size 3 bow. Build up the bow onto the bootie attaching with glue. Spray bows with pearl lustre.

12   Colour 100g of modelling paste pink for the flannel. Roll out thinly on trex and cut out a 12cm square. Fold in half twice. Mark 2 lines with a stitch wheel 7.5mm from cut edges. Mark small lines between with a dresden tool.

13   Colour 50g mexican paste lilac. Cut out 4 small pieces of paste for ribbon loops and leave to dry over a paintbrush handle. Colour 2 size 15 balls of modelling paste pink. Shape 2 mittens from pattern (p34). Smooth and round edges. Mark thumb with stitch wheel. Mark vertical lines first, then the knitted pattern between with the dresden tool. Attach a strip of paste across top of mittens 2cm wide. Crimp edges.

14   Roll out lilac mexican paste. Emboss with quilt and cut out bib (p34). Cut out a strip 1cm side to fit around edge of bib and frill using the veining tool. Attach to bib and mark with stitch wheel. Spray with pearl.

15   Lay bib, booties and mittens on to cake. Make small slits with a knife to push ribbons into top of mittens. Make and attach small bows to the mittens. Make and attach size 3 bow to bib. Dust ribbons and bows with snowflake.

16   Shape socks in modelling paste (p34) using a size 14 ball for each. Mark heel and toe with the stitch wheel and dresden tool. Roll out a strip of paste thinly and cut 2 strips 3cm wide to fit across the top of each sock. Mark knitted pattern as before. Cut out and attach a small bow to one then spray with pearl lustre.

17   Cut out a gift tag and two seperate loops in mexican paste so when dry they can be attached at an angle. Dry gift tag over some crumpled paper.

18   Lay socks and flannel on cake. Roll out thin pieces of modelling paste to attach between items on top of cake. They can be folded, draped over cake edge and placed anywhere that needs filling between models. When happy with arrangement attach all to top of cake with royal icing.

19   Soften white sugarpaste with water. Place in a piping bag and pipe between items spreading and stippling to resemble towelling. Colour a little pink to match flannel and repeat.

20   Roll out mexican paste thinly on a greased board. Cut out large teddy, small teddy, duck and blocks. Dust and paint before attaching to cake. Dust gift tag loops. Write message on gift tag with a food colouring pen. Attach gift tag placing a small piece of modelling paste as the knot for the bow. Push loops into knot and support until dry.

Teddy in Bootie

25.5cm (10in) Square and two 12.5cm (5in) round sponge cakes, 35.5cm (14in) round board, 900g (2lb) Baby Blue Regalice sugarpaste, 454g (1lb) buttercream, 340g (8oz) white sugarpaste, 113g (4oz) brown sugarpaste (Bullrush SK), Mexican paste (p1), a little royal icing, edible glue (p1), Trex.

Paste Colour: Black (SK)

Powder Colours: Flesh, Wedgewood, Pale Lilac and Snowflake Lustre (SK)

Small sharp knife, skewers or satay sticks, E.T. lower case alphabet set (PC), stitch wheel (PME), crimper - single closed curve serrated 2cm, fine paintbrush.

1 For the ribbon roll out Mexican paste and cut out 8 pieces measuring $^3/_4$" by 1". Using letters, emboss with a, b, or c on each and run stitches along top and bottom edge with quilting wheel. Paint the letters with powder colour and Isopropyl Alcohol. Brush over with Snowflake lustre. Leave to dry over a paintbrush handle or similar.

2 Cover the cake board with white sugarpaste and immediately emboss with a, b, & c from alphabet set. Crimp edges.

3 Using the template (page 36) cut out two bootie shapes from the 10" square sponge cake. Cut a small piece of sponge from trimmings to help shape toe. Sandwich together with buttercream. Attach on the two 5" round cakes at heel end using more buttercream (fig 1). Push in two satay sticks at heel end and two along the bootie. Keep the ends showing. Now shape the sponge as shown in the picture, not forgetting to remove sponge from inside top of bootie to accept teddy. Remove satay sticks (fig 2).

4 Spread buttercream all over the bootee and cover with baby blue icing. Bring the excess icing to the back of the cake and trim off in a straight line. This will be the first line

of your embossed pattern. Grease hands lightly with Trex and smooth all over the icing. Crimp a line to mark the sole. Also crimp around the open top edge and the top of the shoe. Cover in clingfilm. Use the pointed end of the Quilting wheel to mark the pattern on the bootie. Keep the icing covered as you work and only uncover as much as you need to work on. This is to prevent the icing from drying out before embossing is completed. First mark the lines down the bootie, then add the small stitches (see diagram 1 & 2)

fig 1

5 Attach pieces of ribbon made earlier around ankle of bootie. Push in and stick with royal icing. Cut out Mexican paste to make bow loops and ties. Emboss with letters and add stitching to match the ribbon pieces. Colour as instruction 1. Form loops and ties to make a bow and attach to front of bootie. Support loops until dry.

6 Model the teddy's body from the brown sugarpaste. Place into the bootie. Make his arms and stick them in place, then the head. Stick on black sugarpaste eyes and nose. Fill a small piping bag with brown royal icing to match the teddy colour. Tear off the end to make a hole roughly the size of a 2-3 piping tube. Pipe on to the teddy and using a damp paintbrush brush the fur in the direction it would grow.

7 Paint in the letters on the cake board to match the ribbon. Brush over the iced board with Snowflake lustre.

fig 2

diagram 1

diagram 2

Barbeque

20cm (8in) Square cake marzipanned, 28cm (11in) cake board, 1.3kg (3lb) Icecraft sugarpaste, 50g (2oz) marzipan, flower paste, royal icing, edible glue (p1) isopropyl alcohol, confectioners varnish (optional)

Paste Colours: **Spruce Green, Navy, Red, Paprika, Pink, Dark Brown, Black (SF).**

Powder Colours: **Snowdrop, Gingko, Dark Brown, Kingfisher, Strawberry, Burnt Orange, Yellow (SC), Silver (SK)**

Small daisy / marguerite plunger cutter (PME), stitch wheel / dresden tool (PME), mouth tool (Jem), bone tool, fine paintbrush, dusting brush, soft sponge.

1 Colour 900g of sugarpaste green. Place cake on board, cover with green sugarpaste, then ice the board. Mix a little isopropyl alcohol with green powder colour and paint tufts of grass randomly all over cake. Paint a thicker line of grass along lower edge on top of cake. Paint some circles of white petals for flowers then add a yellow dot in the centre.

2 Roll out white flower paste and cut out approximately 44 small daisies. Press into sponge to give shape. Leave to dry. Colour some royal icing green and place in a piping bag. Trim the point of the bag to a 'V' shape and pipe pairs of leaves around base of cake leaving a small gap to attach daisies. Attach a daisy between two leaves. Paint daisy centres yellow.

3 Colour 65g of sugarpaste grey, 50g blue, 45g red and 30g of marzipan flesh.

4 Using the size guide (p1) shape shoes each from a size 10 ball of grey sugarpaste. Make oval shapes and mark with a dresden tool. Roll a sausage 12.5cm long from a size 16 ball of blue sugarpaste. Bend in half to form 2 legs. Trim straight at hem of each leg. Mark with a stitch wheel and dresden tool. Dust seams and creases with a flat dusting brush and blue powder. Attach jeans and shoes to cake with glue.

5 Shape body from a size 15 ball of red sugarpaste. Narrow slightly at shoulders. Attach to cake then mark neck and hem with the dresden tool and stitch wheel. Shape sleeves each from a size 10. Attach to cake and mark as before. Shape arms each from a size 11 ball of marzipan. Trim straight at the top to attach to sleeve. Thin at wrist and flatten for hand, mark fingers then curve slightly. Bend and crease at elbows then attach to cake with palms of hands upwards. Roll a thin sausage of flower paste 4cm long for fork handle and leave to dry. Colour a size 8 ball of marzipan brown and shape for the bottle. Attach to hand with glue. Roll a thin piece of flower paste and cut out a label 1.5cm x 1cm. Attach to bottle. When label is dry write the word 'Beer' using a food colouring pen. Confectioners varnish may be painted on the bottle if you wish.

6 Roll out thin flower paste and cut out an apron measuring 6.5cm by 5cm (shoulder straps can be cut out at the same time or added later). Attach to figure and add a tie to each side of waist.

7 Roll a small flattened ball of marzipan for neck and attach to body. Head is shaped from a size 13 ball of marzipan. Make slightly egg shaped and flatten a little in eye area. Attach a small teardrop shaped nose and 2 small balls of paste for ears. Press a bone tool into front of ears and into side of head. Emboss the mouth with the mouth tool pressing down slightly to give a big smile. Press a bone tool into the face for the eyes and fill with small balls of white flower paste. Mark eyebrows with the mouth tool.

8 Dust cheeks with a little pink powder. Paint eyes with an appropriate powder colour mixed with isopropyl alcohol. Paint eyelashes. Dip a cocktail stick into black paste colour and mark pupils. Soften a little sugarpaste with water (p1) and colour for hair. Use a paintbrush to apply to head. Flatten a size 8 ball of white sugarpaste and attach to top of head. For the hat top, shape an oval from a size 12 ball of paste, flatten slightly and indent around edges with a Dresden tool. Attach to cake.

9 Shape 6 sausages from marzipan. Leave to dry. From a size 16 ball of grey sugarpaste make a wedge shape for barbeque. Pinch it out towards the front and up at the back. Colour some flower paste darker grey. For the grill roll out an oval piece of paste and cut a leaf shape to measure approximately 6.5cm long x 4cm wide with a point at each end. Attach to top of barbeque trimming to fit. Mark lines across top with a knife or dresden tool.

10 Roll out grey flower paste thinly and cut 3 strips measuring 4cm x 5mm. Make 2 wheels and add a small flattened ball of grey sugarpaste to each. Attach legs, wheels and bar between legs to cake with glue. Attach barbeque. Roll tiny pieces of flower paste for handles and attach. Paint a little red and orange powder into grill and a little silver for smoke behind the barbeque onto the cake. Attach sausages to barbeque and one to fork. Dust with a little brown powder.

11 Colour a little royal icing grey and pipe the word 'Cheers!'. Mix isopropyl alcohol with silver powder and paint the barbeque, the fork and 'Cheers!'.

30.5cm (12in) Square sponge cake, 30.5cm x 35cm (12in x 18in) oblong board, 1.8kg (4lb) Regalice sugarpaste (of which 400g coloured blue and 400g coloured green), 227g (8oz) modelling paste (p1) (of which 110g coloured lilac), 454g (1lb) buttercream, isopropyl alcohol, edible glue (p1).

Paste Colours: **Rose** (SK)

Powder Colours: **Daffodil, Snowflake** (SK), **Chocolate, Peach, Colonial Rose** (EA).

Basketweave and mini basketweave embossers (PC), LA1 lace cutter (OP), no.1 piping nozzle, star nozzle, paintbrushes size 00,0,1, dusting brushes, stitch wheel, a daisy cutter, E.T. upper & lower case alphabet sets (PC), size guide (CC).

1   Cover approximately ½ the board in blue sugarpaste, the remainder of the board in green sugarpaste. Cut a wavy line across the board where the two colours overlap. Remove excess green paste. Peel back green paste and remove excess blue paste. Stick green paste back in place. Place the rabbit template (p--) on the board. Place the star tube onto your index finger and emboss all green paste around and up to the template. Emboss marks very closely together so as to look like grass. Remove the template. Continue to emboss the unmarked paste a little further, this will ensure the grass pattern will be visible all the way around the finished rabbit.

2   Cut out the rabbit cake using the template provided (p36). Shape sides all the way around, except along bottom of the cake i.e. the hem of the dress. Trim away small amount of sponge cake from sides, tapering inward and down to the board. Cut the arm and the lower half of the face (fig 1), shaping to form a pointed nose. Attach the face onto the main cake using buttercream. Cover the whole rabbit with buttercream, then white Regalice. The arm is iced separately. Mark the pointed end of the arm to make a paw and

attach later. Place the cake onto the iced board.

3   Petal dust the rabbit's face and outside of ears very lightly with the Bulrush powder. Mix the bulrush with alcohol and paint in the fur and face. Brush rose powder into the ears. For nose, use a no. 7 ball of white sugar paste. Flatten slightly into a triangular shape. Attach with edible glue and dust pink.

4   With the lilac modelling paste roll a size 16 ball (using the size guide). Roll into a sausage approximately 7"(18cms.) long to form the hat base. Thin out and point the ends, then curve and position on the head. Pinch the front of the hat base, flattening down the back towards the ears to form the hat shape.

5   Using the size guide (p1) and lilac modelling paste roll a no 16 & 14 ball together into an oblong measuring 10"x 4" (approx. 25 x 10 cms.). Emboss the mini basketweave on in two rows of three. Trim edges, then attach to the hat shape making sure to fold down front edge of hat, along and around underside of hat base. Crimp around front edge of hat. Paint behind the hat and ears down to the board in appropriate colours.

6   Colour a no 12 ball of modelling paste Rose and roll out strips. Cut out the bow pieces. Use the Quilting Wheel to mark the stitches. Fold and stick in place.

7   Roll a long white sausage from a no 15 ball of white sugarpaste and stick along hem of dress on the board. Make layers of garrett frills, bending the straight edge to stick them to the flat part of the cake and resting them on the roll of sugarpaste. Repeat until the frills are level with the top of the dress.

8   For the skirt, roll out 6ozs (170g) of modelling paste and cut into a 15"x 5"(38 x 12.5 cms.) oblong. Check the length against your cake and gather up the waist very

slightly. Stick along the waistline. Drape the skirt over the cake top and sides.

9   For the apron roll out 3ozs (85g) of modelling paste into an 8"x 4"(approx. 20 x 10 cms.) oblong. Cut the hem with the lace cutter. Cut a pattern with a no 2 nozzle along the hem. Gather up the top edge and stick to dress. Press down to secure. Make ½ a bow and mark with stitches and stick left of waistband.

10   Make the basket the same way as the hat. Roll a sausage from a no15 ball and stick to cake. Roll out a no16 ball to a 6"x 2" (approx 15x5cms.) oblong. Emboss with the large basketweave embosser. Stick in place, making sure the top of the embossed paste lays a little higher than the base, to accept baby bunnies. Curve the sides down. Make left paw from a ball of sugar paste to match the right paw. Dust and paint both paws. Stick the arm on to the cake with buttercream. Attach the left paw with sugar glue. Roll sausages of pink paste and twist them into ropes for the handles and stick in place.

11   Cut out the collar and cuff, crimp the edge and stick in place.

12   Using a fine paintbrush paint on flowers and leaves using powder colours and Isopropyl Alcohol.

13   Using Snowflake Lustre dust the pinny, cuffs and collar.

14   Model the babies heads from no 11 balls of brown sugarpaste, their ears are no.7 each. The bodies are various sizes depending on their position. Stick into place. Paint in faces.

15   Using modelling paste cut out two daisies for each letter of the name. Soften petals slightly and stick two together. Emboss each letter into the flower then gently place into foil cups and leave to dry. Dust edges of petals with pink powder. Paint letters with

yellow powder and alcohol. Add extra green colour to green sugarpaste, soften with water and mix until smooth. Fill a piping bag and cut a small hole in the end. Pipe a curved line long enough to attach daisies. Stick daisies in place then cut a small 'V' at the end of the bag. Pipe leaves behind each daisy.

Fig 1

25cm (10in) marzipanned rich fruit cake placed on a 36cm (14in) cake board, 1.8kg Icecraft sugarpaste, royal icing coloured grey, piping gel, 1 pot each of white, hint of green, hint of lilac, hint of pink, hint of lemon and red Magic Sparkles (BK), edible glue (p1), isopropyl alcohol, Mexican paste, Trex.

Paste Colours: **Ice Blue, Egg Yellow, Ruby, Spruce Green, Red Extra, Violet, Black (SF).**

Powder Colours: **Silver, Moonbeams Ruby and Jade (SK), Primrose, Sunflower (SC).**

2cm (³/₄ in) plain closed curve crimper, small glass cutter (PC), fruit set (PC), no. 2 piping nozzle, dresden tool (PME), cutting wheel (PME), scriber (optional), paintbrushes, non stick rolling pin and board.

1 Ice cake and crimp around top edge immediately. Ice board and crimp around edge.

2 Trace glass and umbrella patterns on p33 and cut out. Colour 5 pieces of Mexican paste different colours for drinks and umbrella. Colour a small piece grey for straws. Roll paste out very thinly on trex and use the cutting wheel to cut out shapes. Lay patterns on top of cake positioning correctly and mark with a scriber or cocktail stick. Remove patterns then attach drinks with glue. Attach straws. Mark umbrella with a Dresden tool and attach.

3 Roll out white Mexican paste and cut a circle measuring approximately 2.5cm diameter. Mix isopropyl alcohol with powder colours and paint to resemble a slice of lemon. Attach to cake with a little royal icing.

4 Colour a little Mexican paste red. Grease a non stick rolling board and the strawberry and cherry cutters with trex. Roll paste out thinly and cut out 1 pair of cherries and 2 strawberries. Cut out cherry leaves and stems and a calyx for each strawberry in green Mexican paste. Attach and leave to dry.

5 Cut out 12 small glasses – 4 each of pink, yellow and blue. Attach to sides of cake. Dust top of glasses and stems with snowflake. Brush the front of the glasses with glue and attach fine magic sparkles (p1) in the appropriate colours.

6 Place grey royal icing in a piping bag with a no.2 nozzle. Pipe outlines of glasses, bubbles, lettering, a small plain shell around base of cake and crimping around edge of cake board. Mix silver powder colour with isopropyl alcohol and paint all grey piping and straws.

7 Place piping gel in a bag and fill glasses. Leave to dry for a few hours. Attach magic sparkles to top of two glasses. Dust strawberries with moonbeams ruby. Cover cherries with red magic sparkles. Dust leaves and calyx with jade. Attach fruit to glasses with royal icing.

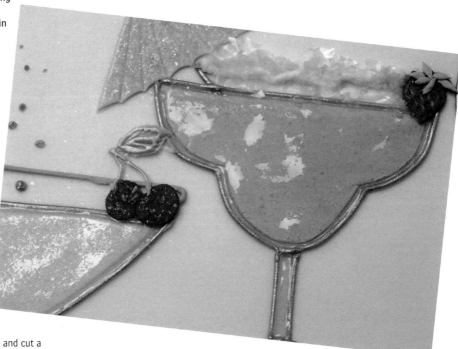

Baby in Scales

20cm (8in) marzipanned cake placed on a 28cm (11in) board, 1.1kg (2½lb) Icecraft sugarpaste, small piece of marzipan coloured with a little paprika and pink, small piece of modelling paste, royal icing, mexican paste, black food colouring pen, blue Magic Sparkles (BK), edible glue (p1), isopropyl alcohol, Trex.

Paste Colours: Ice Blue, Black, Brown

Dust Colours: Silver, Bronze Lustre, Snowflake (SK), Speedwell Blue, Rose Pink, Caramel (SC)

Mini basketweave embosser (PC) teddy cutters from make a cradle set (PC), rabbits embosser from set 9 spring countryside (HP), embosser from set 1 small floral (HP), mouth embosser / veining tool (Jem), bow cutter no.2 (Jem), no.1 & no.2 piping nozzles, 4.5cm circle cutter, paint brushes.

1 Colour 1kg of sugarpaste pale blue and ice cake and board. Emboss board with small teddy, rabbits and small embosser. Brush iced board with snowflake lustre. Mix isopropyl alcohol with silver powder and paint teddies and rabbits.

2 Soften a little blue sugarpaste with water (p1) and using a no.1 nozzle, pipe a small plain shell around base of cake.

3 Colour a small piece of mexican paste brown and a larger piece grey. Roll out both pieces on a board greased with trex. Grease teddy cutters and cut out a small brown bear and 4 larger grey bears. Leave to dry. Dust grey bears with silver powder and brown bear with caramel. Use a fine paintbrush and black paste colour to paint small teddy's eyes and nose.

4 Using the size guide (p1) colour a size 15 ball of sugarpaste grey. Remove 3 small balls of paste (2 for feet, 1 for under basket). Shape scales from pattern on p32, attach to cake, add feet and add other piece to top centre of scales. Cut out a circle of mexican paste and attach to front of scales. Cut out the arrow (p32) in mexican paste and leave to dry.

5 Trace the pattern for the basket (p32). Shape a wedge of sugarpaste for the basket to fit around – but slightly narrower for the baby to sit in, and attach to cake. Roll out brown mexican paste and emboss with the mini basketweave. Cut out basket. Dust basket with bronze powder then attach over wedge.

6 Roll out a strip of mexican paste and cut to measure 10cm x 2cm. Dust with snowflake lustre. Brush inside top edge of basket with glue then place blanket over edge folding a little to fit.

7 Roll a size 9 ball of marzipan for baby's body. Flatten slightly, mark a belly button and attach inside basket. From a size 7 ball of sugarpaste, shape a nappy and attach. Roll 2 sausages of marzipan each from

a size 7. Shape leg and foot then mark creases at back of knee. Flatten slightly at thigh and attach one under nappy and one over. Roll 10 tiny balls of marzipan for toes. Attach in size order to feet.

8 Shape the left arm and hand from a size 5 and attach tucking under body slightly. Bend hand back slightly and attach teddy. Shape other arm from a size 6 placing hand over teddy.

9 Shape head from a size 11 , flattening slightly before attaching. Mark mouth with the mouth tool. Dust cheeks with a little pink powder. Add a tiny ball of marzipan for the nose and small balls for ears. Press the end of a paintbrush handle into front of ears.

10 Indent for eyes with the paintbrush handle. Insert small balls of white mexican paste into eyes. Paint pale blue. Mark pupils with the tip of a cocktail stick dipped in black paste colour. Use a fine paintbrush to paint eyelashes and eyebrows.

11 Soften a little brown sugarpaste with water (p1) and dab on top of head with a paintbrush to make hair stand up.

12 Pipe the word 'baby' and the name on to the cake using a no.2 nozzle with grey royal icing. Mark scales with the food colouring pen and attach arrow. Mix isopropyl alcohol and silver powder to paint teddies, rabbits, scales, arrow and lettering.

13 Colour a little mexican paste blue then cut out and attach a bow to scales. Brush with glue then cover with magic sparkles.

Baby   8lb 1oz   James

Line Dancers

20cm (8in) Square fruit cake, 28cm (11in) cake drum, 900g (2lb) marzipan, 900g (2lb) Regalice sugarpaste coloured brown (Bullrush SK), 380g (14oz) marzipan with 1½ tsp of gum tragacanth added and coloured as follows:- 10g Bulrush, 18og Bluebell, 50g Terracotta, 30g Flesh, 70g Bridal satin double cream, 40g red (all SK colours), 113g of sugarpaste coloured with Holly / Ivy paste colour (SK), 227g modelling paste coloured cream with Sunflower paste colour (SK), edible supports (p1), edible glue (p1), Trex.

Paste Colours: **Holly / Ivy, Sunflower (SK).**

Powder Colours: **Bullrush, Silver, Flesh (SK).**

Baber Folk Food Paints: **Red & Cornflower (SK).**

White Hologram glitter (EA), watermark taffeta effect rolling pin (HP), no.2 piping nozzle, star piping nozzle, large and small sharp knives, size guide (CC), stitch wheel (PME), small star cutter, fine paintbrush, flat dusting brush.

1 Marzipan & ice the fruit cake using the brown sugarpaste. Immediately roll the taffeta pin on the top and sides of the cake. Use a large knife to mark out the boards of wood, and use the no 2 tube to mark two nails either side of joins.

2 Leave to dry, (preferably overnight). Use a flat dusting brush with a little Bulrush powder to highlight the grain of the wood.

3 Ice the board with green paste. Randomly press the star tube into the paste to give grass effect. Soften some green paste with water until it is of piping consistency. Pipe fine blades of grass around base of cake (you do not need a piping tube).

4 Measure the height and width of your cake sides using the size guide. For cake drapes roll out cream modelling paste thinly. Grease the board you are working on and the top of the paste so as to slow down drying time. Cut to size. Emboss star cutter (see opposite page). Fold paste over and stick down a small hem along top edge of reverse side. Paint edible glue along top edge of cake and sides of panels. Pinch and fold sides and attach to cake. Paint in stars with the Baber paints. Mark small balls of modelling paste and attach to corners.

Men...

1 For each boot roll a no 7 ball using the size guide. Point the toe, flatten sole, and shape heel by using the pointed end of the quilting tool (see fig1 and fig2).

2 Use a no 14 ball for each pair of jeans. Roll to a sausage shape, flatten slightly, cut up the middle and smooth the legs. Use the quilting tool to mark stitch lines on the jeans. Turn out the left leg. Stick on the boots, pointing the left boot to the side.

3 The shirt body is a size 12 ball of Terracotta. Shape and mark the button band, then the buttons with the no 2 tube. Attach to the jeans. Use a no 7 for each sleeve. Hollow out the sleeve edge with a ball tool or paintbrush.

4 The hands are each a no 2 ball rolled to a teardrop shape. Pull out and form thumb and emboss thumbnail with a no 2 tube. Use a very small piece of blue marzipan for belt loop. Roll out very thinly in the palm of your hand and stick around thumb. Attach the hand into the shirt sleeve. Stick the hand to the top of the jeans first and then the sleeve to the shirt.

5 Cut out a shirt collar and stick on. If required paint a check pattern on shirt using Baber food paint. When dry, roll out two pieces of black marzipan to make a tie. Attach to shirt collar. Paint the ends and the top silver.

6 Use a no 11 ball for head. Cut mouth shape and stick on a small nose. Roll two very tiny balls into 'c' shapes and stick on for ears. Paint eyes and eyebrows. It is best at this stage to leave the figure to dry overnight before attaching the hat and hair and positioning on cake.

7 Pipe on the hair. The hats are made with a no 10 or 11 ball, depending on what size you prefer. Roll a ball then press in your finger. Start to work on the hat brim (see hat 1). Try not to squash or fill in hole made by finger. Pinch and shape the top of the hat (see hat 2) then stick it to your figures head. Fold up the sides to get a good 'Stetson' shape. Cut out a star in red or blue and leave to dry. Paint with sugar glue then dip into White Hologram and lift out on a knife. Leave to dry and then stick to front of hat.

Ladies...

1 Girls boots are each a no 10 ball. Make as for man, but pull up the leg and press in a few creases at front of ankle (see figs 1 and 2).

2 The skirts are a no 14. When you shape the skirt hollow out slightly, so the top of the boot sits inside. Mark seams with the quilting tool, then stick on boots.

3 Mould the body from a size 12 and stick to skirt. Cut out back and sides of denim jacket from thinly rolled marzipan. Mark on stitching. The sleeves are no 7 and are made the same way as the mens. Make hands and belt loops as for men.

4 Use a triangle of red marzipan for back of scarf, and small pieces to make a knot and ties for the front.

5 Paint pattern on boots with Baber food paint.

6 Make head and hat as on men's figures. Attach to cake using royal icing, supporting with styrofoam until completely dry.

Easter

20cm (8in) Rich fruit cake marzipanned and iced (in Icecraft sugarpaste) placed on a 28cm (11in) iced board, 140g (4¹/₂oz) sugarpaste, Mexican paste, edible glue (p1), isopropyl alcohol.

Paste Colours: Dark Brown, Mint Green, Grape Violet, Peach, Egg Yellow, Spruce Green (SF).

Powder Colours: Caramel, Snowdrop, Primrose, Sunflower (SC), Moonbeams Topaz and Jade (SK).

Spray colours: Blue, Green (PME).

Cutting wheel (PME), stitch wheel (PME), large alphabet set (PC), mini basketweave & mini quilting embossers (PC), daffodil embosser from small floral set (HP), rabbits embosser from countryside set (HP), mouth tool (Jem), small calyx cutter 1cm (or a star cutter), bone tool, sponge pad, 3 white stamens, paintbrushes.

1. Spray top half of cake and board blue and lower halves green. Move the can before you press the spray button so you get an even covering (you could practice on a spare piece of icing first).

2. Trace the letter patterns on p32. Colour some small pieces of Mexican paste then cut out letters using the patterns and a cutting wheel. Finish each letter as follows: 'E' - emboss with rabbits and small flower, mix powder colour with isopropyl alcohol then paint rabbits and flowers. Dust with topaz. 'a'- emboss with the basketweave then dust with Jade. 'S'- Cut out with the cutter from the large alphabet set then mark with the stitch wheel. 't' - Emboss with the quilting embosser then dust with topaz. 'e'- emboss with the daffodil, paint then dust with topaz. 'R'- Cut out with the cutter from the alphabet set then dust with jade. Leave all letters to dry.

3. To make small daffodils, colour some Mexican paste pale yellow, yellow, cream and peach. Cut out a calyx then press the centre with a bone tool on a sponge pad. Take a tiny ball of paste and press over the end of a paintbrush handle and hollow out. Attach to centre of calyx and leave to dry. You will need to make approximately 40 in several colour combinations.

4. Mix a little water with some green paste colours. Paint grass from bottom of cake up side of cake and out towards board edge. Paint grass across top of cake just below half way and a little under where rabbit will be positioned.

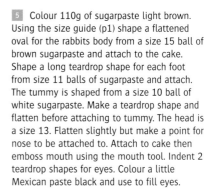

5. Colour 110g of sugarpaste light brown. Using the size guide (p1) shape a flattened oval for the rabbits body from a size 15 ball of brown sugarpaste and attach to the cake. Shape a long teardrop shape for each foot from size 11 balls of sugarpaste and attach. The tummy is shaped from a size 10 ball of white sugarpaste. Make a teardrop shape and flatten before attaching to tummy. The head is a size 13. Flatten slightly but make a point for nose to be attached to. Attach to cake then emboss mouth using the mouth tool. Indent 2 teardrop shapes for eyes. Colour a little Mexican paste black and use to fill eyes.

6. Shape arms each from a size 8 ball of sugarpaste. Attach the large letter 'E' to the rabbit. Attach arms to hold letter. Shape ears each from a size 8 ball of sugarpaste. Make a long teardrop shape then hollow with a bone tool. Dust inside ear with a little pink powder and attach to rabbit. Bend one ear forward.

7. Soften a little white and brown sugarpaste with water (p1) and place in piping bags. Pipe over rabbit spreading with a damp paintbrush. Dab at icing to give fur effect. Cut the heads off 3 stamens and cut in half. Push 3 into each cheek. Shape a small nose from pale pink sugarpaste and attach. Paint a small white highlight into each eye.

8. Attach letters across top of cake with softened sugarpaste. Colour some royal icing green and pipe flower stems and long leaves below the letter 'a' and after the letter 'R'. Pipe grass around base of cake and out onto board over painted grass. Pipe sections of leaves and stems at intervals around cake sides. Attach groups of the same coloured flowers to stems.

9. At the front of the cake on the side, shape and attach a group of rabbits. Attach feet, followed by bodies, ears, heads then a tail.

Rudolf's Slippers

One sponge cake baked in a two pint pudding basin, two sponge cakes baked in ³/₄ pint pudding basins, 30.5cm (12in) round cake drum, 454g (1lb) Regalice coloured with Holly / Ivy paste colour (SK), 1.360kg (3lb) Regalice coloured with Bulrush paste colour (SK), 227g (8oz) sugarpaste for hat and slippers, 450g (1lb) buttercream, small amount of royal icing, mexican paste (p1), ¹/₂ tsp of gum tragacanth, a chocolate tea cake, Christmas Sparkle (EA), isopropyl alcohol, Trex.

Powder Colours: Gold, Silver, Rainforest, Poinsettia (SK).

E.T. upper and lower case alphabet sets (PC), gift tag cutter (PC), mini holly, ivy and mistletoe set (PC), stitch wheel (PME), fine paintbrush, small curved nail scissors.

1 Trim the largest cake into a rounder body shape. Coat large cake in buttercream and cover with brown sugarpaste. Grease hands lightly with Trex and smooth over cake. Use the scissors to snip icing to mark fur.

2 Place gum tragacanth on work surface and knead into 5ozs (140g) of brown sugarpaste. Shape into a round disc about ³/₄" or 2cm thick. Attach neck to body with royal icing.

3 Sandwich the two smaller sponge cakes together with buttercream to form head. Cover the head with buttercream and ice with brown icing. Mark on fur as above. Leave front of head smooth and unsnipped. Snout and eyes etc will be attached later (see step 13).

4 Ice board with the dark green sugarpaste and emboss with the Holly embosser. Leave to dry then paint outlines only with gold powder and alcohol. Keep colour very thin. Touch outline with loaded brush. Colour will run along rest of outline. The berries are painted with red powder mixed with a touch of gold powder.

5 Carefully lift Rudolph's body on to the board.

6 Model two large and four very small antlers from very pale bulrush coloured mexican paste. Leave to dry.

7 Colour 6ozs sugarpaste cream, divide in two and shape slippers by first rolling each piece into a ball. Elongate each ball and pinch up the top at the front. Make a hole in the back to fit leg. Mark a sole and paint pattern on slippers with red and green powder colours mixed with alcohol. Then position on board sticking in place with royal icing.

8 Model each leg from 4ozs (113g) of brown sugarpaste. Position the leg onto the body and into the slippers. Stick in place with royal icing and mark on fur with scissors.

9 Attach Rudolph's head with brown sugar paste softened with water.

10 Roll out red sugarpaste and cut out a collar to fit Rudolph's neck. Mark with the quilting wheel. Stick in place. Roll a ball of paste for bell. Mark with a cocktail stick and stick in place with royal icing. When dry paint silver.

11 Model each front leg from 3ozs (85g) of sugarpaste. Stick in place and mark on fur. Model hooves from light Bulrush mexican paste and stick in place.

12 Make two small reindeer heads from sugarpaste and attach one to each slipper. Push in antlers and support until dry. Paint on faces.

13 Complete Rudolph's face by attaching chocolate tea cake to form snout. Use royal icing for sticking. Cut out two sugarpaste teardrop shapes for eyes and stick in place. Pipe or paint in eyes. Pipe on eyebrows and mouth and attach a red sugarpaste nose. Cut out two ¹/₂ circles and position for eyelids.

14 For hat, roll out 6ozs (170g) red sugarpaste into a half circle. Wrap around head and pull top point over to one side. Use either sugarpaste or royal icing for fur trim and pompom. Push antlers into place.

15 On a lightly greased non-stick board roll out red Mexican paste. Grease gift tag cutter and press onto paste. Press only at the bow end. Remove cutter. Emboss name using alphabet cutters. With a knife cut out and extend length of gift tag around embossed name, ensuring that cut lines meet up with lines previously cut at bow end. Lift tag and place on sponge pad to dry. Paint over the bow and embossed name with sugar glue and sprinkle with Christmas sparkle. Lift tag and gently shake off any excess. Use a dry brush to remove any further excess. Attach tag to cake with sugar glue.

Baby in Scales, Page 24

Butterfly, Page 10

Easter Cake, Page 28

Cocktails, Page 22

(Top of glass)

Patterns

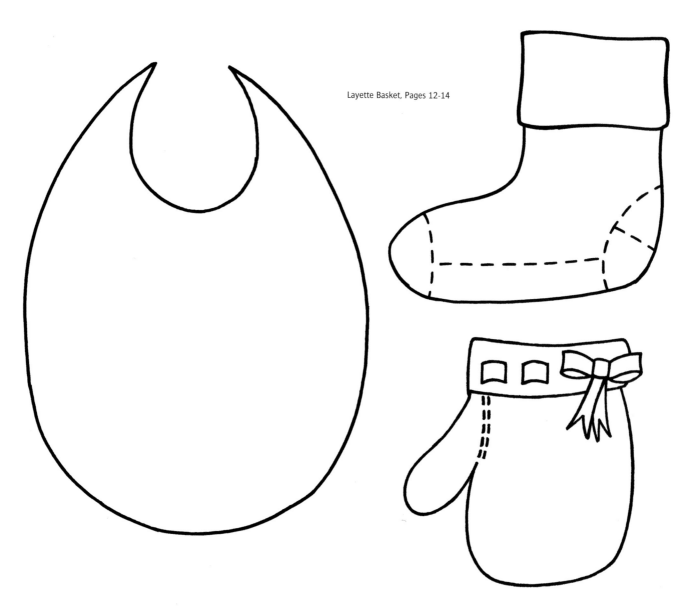

Layette Basket, Pages 12-14

18th Birthday, Page 8

Patterns

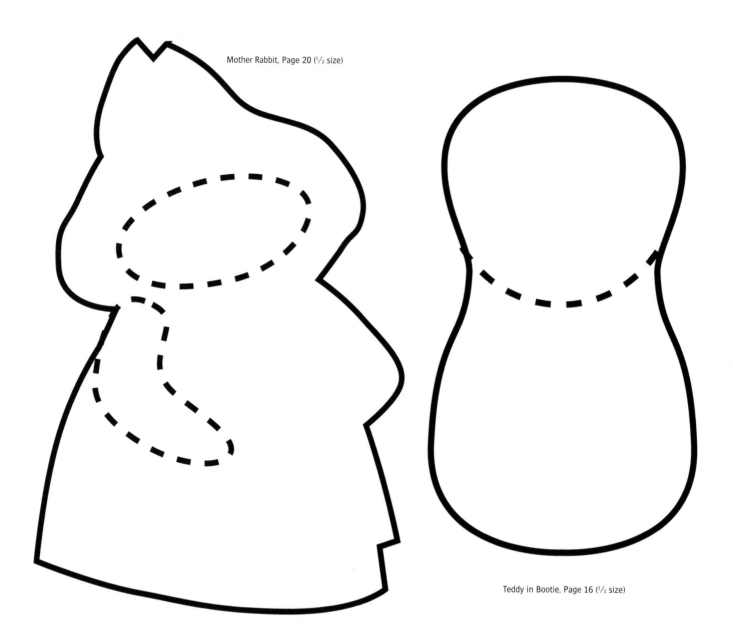

Mother Rabbit, Page 20 ($^1\!/_2$ size)

Teddy in Bootie, Page 16 ($^1\!/_2$ size)